DOMINO GAMES AND PUZZLES

A set of dominoes will open up a
whole new world of fun and
fascination. With a set of dominoes
you can put boredom right behind
you and never have another dull
moment.

This book contains over fifty games
you can play with dominoes . . . have
fun!

3 cde

DOMINO GAMES AND PUZZLES

GYLES BRANDRETH

Illustrated by Colin Mier

TRANSWORLD PUBLISHERS LTD

DOMINO GAMES AND PUZZLES

A CAROUSEL BOOK 0 552 54087 0

PRINTING HISTORY
Carousel edition published 1975

Corgi Books are published by
Transworld Publishers Ltd.,
Cavendish House, 57–59 Uxbridge Road,
Ealing, London W.5.
Made and printed in Great Britain by
Cox & Wyman Ltd., London, Reading and Fakenham

CONTENTS

5

INTRODUCTION

According to the *Oxford English Dictionary*, a wise and wonderful book compiled by wise and wonderful people (I know because I've met them), a domino is 'one of 28 rectangular pieces of ivory, bone or wood, having the under-side black, and the upper equally divided by a line into two squares, each either blank or marked with pips from one to six in number.'

They're right, of course. That's exactly what a domino is, but it's so much more besides. It's a key to a whole new world of fun and fascination. With a set of dominoes, you can put boredom right behind you and never have another dull moment as long as you live. And with this book, you've *got* a set of dominoes, because

9

after you've discovered my Domino Dictionary, my Domino Games, my Domino Solitaire and my Domino Puzzles, you will come across my Do-it-Yourself Domino Set. It's a complete domino-making kit and if you can find 28 empty matchboxes, it will provide you with all the equipment you will need for a lifetime of domino delight

As you can guess, I'm dotty about dominoes. I have been ever since I was given my first set at the age of five and taught a tongue-twister about a simple-minded elephant who was given a set as well. Over the years I haven't learnt how to say 'Dim Dumbo's Dominoes' properly, but I have learnt dozens of delicious domino games and puzzles and I've collected them together in this book in the hope that you will get as much pleasure out of them as I have – and still do.

This book will tell you everything you need to know about *all* the world's most interesting and important domino games. What it won't tell you, I'm sorry to say, is how the '28 rectangular pieces of ivory, bone or wood' came to be called dominoes. Some of the experts say that it's got something to do with the Latin word *dominus*, which means lord or master. Others say it's because one of the pieces, the double-1, looks like the kind of harlequin's mask that's also called a domino. Nobody really knows. And nobody really knows when dominoes were invented or who invented them. In some form or other they have definitely been around for almost 2,000 years, but no one can tell for sure whether it was in Italy or Africa or China or Siam that they first appeared.

What matters is that they *did* appear and that we've got them to enjoy – and enjoy them we must. I make a point of that only because some people do take their dominoes rather seriously and forget it's all only a game. It doesn't really matter if you win or lose. It doesn't really matter if you follow all the rules. All that really matters is that you have fun – and plenty of it.

DOMINO DICTIONARY

In this book you will find an enormous range and variety of domino games and puzzles. Some of them are easy, some of them are difficult. Some of them call for just one player, some of them call for four or five. Some of them are based on well-known card games, some of them are unique. All of them have a language of their own and that's why this book begins with a small Domino Dictionary.

If you've never played cricket, you've probably never heard of a *googly*, a *snick* and a *yorker*. If you've never played tennis, you probably couldn't tell the difference between a *block volley*, a *lob volley* and a *drive volley*. It's the same with dominoes. There are words and phrases that domino enthusiasts love to use and take for granted, but which are totally meaningless if you've never come across them before. With a bit of luck, you should have no difficulty picking up all the correct terms as you go along, but here are a few hints to help you on your way.

The Boneyard

In a game in which all 28 dominoes are not used, the dominoes that are left over when every player has drawn his or her hand, form the boneyard. All the dominoes in the boneyard are left face downwards in a group and this group forms a pool on which players can draw at a later stage, depending, of course, on the rules of the particular game. The boneyard gets its name from the fact that dominoes were once made of bone. Today, it might be a better idea to call the boneyard the graveyard, because modern dominoes look more like little tombstones than bits of bone.

The Discard Pile

In some games and puzzles you take certain dominoes out of play and don't use them again during the particular game or puzzle. Whenever you have to discard a domino, you put it aside with any other discarded dominoes in the Discard Pile.

Drawing Your Hand

No, this has got nothing to do with the sort of hands an artist might draw with a pencil or a paintbrush. When you draw your hand at the beginning of a game of dominoes, you simply take the right number of dominoes from the shuffled pool on the table. If the game then allows you to look at the dominoes you have drawn, you can stand them up on their sides in a row in front of you – making quite sure as you do so that none of the other players can see what you've got in your hand.

Joins that Match

In many domino games and in most domino puzzles you have got to join one domino to another domino on the table and where one domino meets another domino the joins must match. This means, for example, that if there is a 5/2 on the table and you want to join a domino to it you can only join a domino with a 5 in it to the 5-end of the domino on the table or a domino with a 2 in it to the 2-end of the domino on the table.

The Line of Play

In some domino games and puzzles, usually the ones based on card games, *tricks* are taken, but in most others the players build up a long row of dominoes by joining one domino up to another so that the joins match. The row, as it builds up, is called the line of play. Dominoes are joined to the line of play either *with* the line, like this:

or *across* the line, like this:

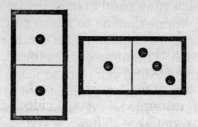

The dominoes that are doubles (the 0/0, 1/1, 2/2, 3/3, 4/4, 5/5 and 6/6) are usually, but not always, played *across* the line of play. The dominoes that aren't doubles (the 21 others) are usually, but not always, played *with* the line of play.

Mistakes

Believe it or not, when you are playing dominoes mistakes *do* happen. For example, you may discover halfway through a game that you began the game by drawing too many dominoes! The moment you make the discovery, you must apologize for your mistake and invite the player sitting on your right to take, sight unseen, one of the dominoes remaining in your hand and place it in either the boneyard or the discard pile. Similarly, if you suddenly realize that you drew too few dominoes to begin with, you can draw an extra one (or ones) from the boneyard or discard pile the moment you make the awful discovery.

Life isn't so easy for you if you make a more serious mistake. For example, if you accidentally play a 4 domino when you should have played a 5, you must withdraw the 4 and replace it if your mistake is discovered before the next player has his turn. However, if the next player has already played, you must leave the 4 where it is and live with the shame of your mistake for the rest of the game!

If ever you make the mistake of playing out of turn, you can withdraw the domino you have played *if* your mistake is discovered before the next player has his turn. If the mistake is only discovered after the next player has played, the domino you have played must stay where it is and play must carry on around the group as if nothing has happened.

Another accident that can easily happen to the best domino player is to knock over one of the dominoes in his hand. If you accidentally expose one of your pieces and it's seen by one of the other players, you must show it to *all* the other players.

Because even domino players are human beings, come what may things will go wrong once in a while. Mistakes aren't encouraged, but they're certainly allowed! Second thoughts, on the other hand, *aren't* allowed. Once you have played a certain domino, you can't change your mind and play another. Unless you have made a definite mistake, every move you make is final – so think *before* you play and you'll have less to regret after!

Order of Play

In some domino games, the first player to make a move is the player who has drawn the double-6. If no one has drawn the 6/6, then the player with the next highest double will be the one to begin. In other domino games – including most of the ones in this book – the first player is chosen by lot. This is done before the hands are drawn and is very simple. The dominoes are shuffled face-downwards and each player draws one domino. The player who gets the domino with most pips on it becomes the first player. If two or more players get dominoes of equal value (for example one gets the 5/5 which counts for 10 and another gets the 6/4 which also counts for 10) those players choose a fresh domino each and whichever has the highest now begins. After the first player has played, play always moves to the left, so the second player will always be the person on the left of the first player, and the third player will always be the person on the left of the second player, and so on.

Pips

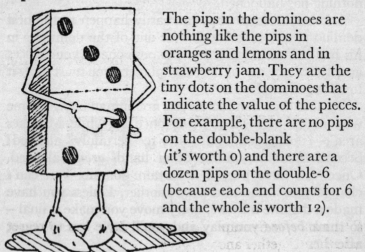

The pips in the dominoes are nothing like the pips in oranges and lemons and in strawberry jam. They are the tiny dots on the dominoes that indicate the value of the pieces. For example, there are no pips on the double-blank (it's worth 0) and there are a dozen pips on the double-6 (because each end counts for 6 and the whole is worth 12).

Scoring

Different domino games have different systems for scoring. In some there is no scoring at all. In others there is a lot of scoring and it is quite complicated. The rules of the game will make it clear how to score in each particular case. Usually it is simply a matter of adding up the pips on the dominoes and, more often than not, it's only the *ends* of the line of play that count. The ends of the line of play are *not* the end dominoes – they are *half* the end dominoes, the half, as you'd expect, that's nearest the end of the line of play. Of course, if there is only one domino on the table, from the point of view of scoring, both ends will be part of the same domino. For example, if the double-5 was the only domino to have been played and you needed to count its worth, you'd have no trouble:

Obviously, it's worth 10. Adding up the score for these two is just as easy:

The 1 and the 6 count as the ends of the line of play and add them together and you get 7.

It's a little different when you get a domino played *across* the line at the end of the line of play, because you are allowed to count all the pips on a domino that's played across the line. For example:

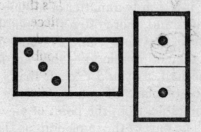

In this situation one end of the line of play is obviously 3, but the other is the double-1, for which both pips score and you get 2, making a combined total for the ends of that particular line of play, of 5.

Getting double value out of a double that's played *across* the line of play only counts, of course, when the double comes at the *end* of the line of play. In this situation, for example,

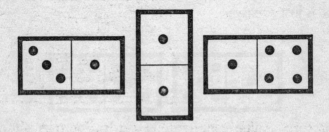

the 3 at one end and the 4 at the other are the scoring ends of the line of play.

The Set

All the games and puzzles in this book are designed for what is officially called the Double-6 Set. It's the traditional 28 piece domino set that everybody uses. It's called the Double-6 Set because, of course, the double-6 (6/6) is the top domino in the set. You *can* get enormous Double-9 and Double-12 Sets, but you don't see them very often nowadays, and every single one of the best-known and most enjoyable domino games and puzzles are meant to be played with the Double-6 Set.

Shuffling

You can't shuffle dominoes like cards. You must shuffle dominoes by laying them face-down on the table and moving them around and around and around so that they get properly jumbled up.

Tricks

When you take a trick at dominoes, it's not like taking a trick to the Magic Circle. Taking a trick at dominoes means winning two or more dominoes by playing a domino that's more powerful than the others played by your opponents. It's something that happens in the domino games based on card games and when to do it and how to do it is explained with the rules of each game.

DOMINO GAMES

Traditional Favourites

First Game

To the millions of miserable people who still haven't discovered the real delights of dominoes and imagine that there is only one domino game, this is that one game. It's called the First Game because it's almost always the very first game that people learn to play when they get a set of dominoes.

For all too many people, it's not only the first domino game they learn: it's also the last – which is why they think it's the only one. As you'll discover as you read this book, there are lots of very different domino games. All of them are more difficult than this one and, to be honest, most of them are more exciting. But since we're still only at the beginning of the book, we'd better begin at the beginning with the First Game. It's fun, it's quick, it's easy – and here are the rules:

1. The first player is chosen by lot.
2. The dominoes are shuffled face downwards. If there are three players, each player now takes 9 dominoes. If there are four players, each player now takes 7 dominoes. If there are five players, each player now takes 5 dominoes. If there are any dominoes left over, as there will be if there are three or five players, the left-over dominoes are put aside and neither used nor looked at during the game.

3. Each player studies his dominoes carefully, but, of course, makes sure that none of the other players can see what he has got in his hand. When all the players are ready, it's time for the first player to make his first move.

4. The aim of the game is to be the first player to get rid of all your dominoes. Bearing this in mind, the first player places any one of his dominoes face-upwards on the table. He now looks again at the dominoes that remain in his hand and sees if he has a second domino that will match his first. One domino matches another if there are the same number of pips on either end of one domino as there are on either end of the other. For example, if the first domino put down is the 5/1, any other domino figuring a 5 or a 1 (including the double-5 or the double-1) will match it. If the first player is able to match his first domino with a second domino, he does so. He lays the second domino next to the first domino, so that the two ends that figure the same number of pips join. He now looks at the dominoes in his hand once more and if he sees a third domino that will match either end of the row of dominoes he has begun to build on the table, he plays it. He goes on doing this *either* until he can no longer play a matching domino *or* until he has played all his dominoes – in which case the game's over and he's won!

5. If the first player doesn't go out during his first turn, when he gets stuck and can no longer play a matching domino, it becomes the second player's turn. He now looks at the dominoes in his hand to see if he has one that will match either of the ends of the two on the table. If he has a matching domino, he plays it and looks at his hand again to see if he has another.

This goes on, either until he wins by going out or until he too gets stuck, when it's the third player's turn.

6. Play passes like this around and around the group until one of the player's manages to get rid of all of his dominoes. He's the outright winner. If it turns out that no one can go out because all the players still have dominoes but cannot match them to the ends of the row on the table, the player with the lowest number of pips on his dominoes is declared the winner.

Ends

Very sensibly, we put the First Game right at the beginning of the book. Just as sensibly, we haven't put
Ends at the end. It's here, right by the First Game, because it's just as easy and really rather similar. It's not as
well known, but it's quite as much fun.

1. When the dominoes have been well shuffled face-
   downwards, each of the four players takes 7.
2. The players all look at their dominoes and the
   player with the double-6 (6/6) begins by putting it
   face-up in the middle of the table.
3. Each player in turn now has to match one end of the
   row of dominoes with one of the dominoes in his
   hand. He can only play one matching domino at a
   time.
4. If a player doesn't have a matching domino when
   it's his turn, he must ask the player sitting on his left
   for one. If that player does have a matching
   domino, he gives it to the player who asked for it.
   The player who asked for it now plays it and it
   becomes the turn of the player who gave him the
   domino.
5. If the player who is asked for a matching domino
   doesn't have one, *he* must ask the player on *his* left
   for one. If that player has one, he gives it to the first
   player, who plays it and it becomes the second
   player's turn.
6. However, if the third player doesn't have the
   matching domino that the second player doesn't
   have and the first player doesn't have either, he then
   asks the fourth player for it. If he has it, he passes it
   to the first player, who plays it, and then the second
   and third players take their turns as usual.
7. If the request for a matching domino goes right

round the group and none of the players has one, the first player who asked for it is then allowed to play *any* domino in his hand.

8. The first player to get rid of all his dominoes is the winner.

Blind Dominoes

This game isn't as old as Blind Man's Buff, nor is it as noisy and exhausting, but it's great fun all the same. And you will find it very relaxing as an interlude between a heavy bout of Muggins and a long session of Concentration, because it doesn't require any skill. With Blind Dominoes, luck is all you need.

1. The first player is chosen by lot.
2. The dominoes are shuffled face-downwards. If there are two or three players, they each now take 7 dominoes. If there are four or five players, they each now take 5 dominoes. The left-over dominoes are put to one side and not touched or looked at for the rest of the game.
3. The players do not look at the dominoes they have

chosen. They simply line them up in a neat row on the table in front of them.

4. The first player begins by turning over the left-hand domino of his row and places it face up in the middle of the table.

5. The second player (who is sitting on the left of the first player) now turns over the left-hand domino of his row. If one of its ends matches one of the ends of the domino that is already in the middle of the table, the second domino is now joined to the first. But if neither end of the domino matches, the second player turns his domino over again and puts it back at the *right-hand* end of his row of dominoes.

6. The next player now turns over the left-hand domino of his row. If it matches either end of the line of play in the middle of the table, he plays it. If it doesn't, he just turns it over again and returns it to the right-hand end of his own row.

7. This goes on around and around the group until one of the players has got rid of all of his dominoes. That player is the winner.

8. If after several rounds it's clear that no one is going to win because no one has a domino that will make a match, the game is declared a *stale-mate*. Nobody wins and you start all over again.

Doubles

Here's a simple domino game that you will enjoy when you're new to the world of dominoes. After you've played Doubles a few times, you'll be ready and eager to have a go at more exciting and difficult versions of the same game, like Round the Clock and Maltese Cross.

1. The first player is chosen by lot.
2. The dominoes are shuffled face-downwards. When there are two, three or four players, each player draws 7 dominoes. When there are five players, each player draws 5 dominoes. The remaining dominoes form the boneyard.
3. The first player plays a double by placing it in the middle of the table. If he hasn't got a double, he must draw from the boneyard until he gets one.
4. The next player must match one end of the first player's double. If he can't, he must draw until he can. The next player must match the other end of the first player's double.
5. The second and third dominoes must now be matched with their doubles and players must either play the right dominoes from their hands or draw from the boneyard until they have the right domino or, when the boneyard is exhausted, pass. At all times the pattern of the line must be: double – matching domino – double – matching domino – double, with doubles alternating with two-figure dominoes.
6. The first player to go out by getting rid of all of his dominoes is the winner.

Round the Clock

Here's a game that gets its name as much from the way the dominoes look on the table as from the fact that it's so exciting you could go on playing it day and night. Whether you decide to play Round the Clock round the clock or not, you will find the game a little more demanding than the First Game and Ends and Blind Dominoes. And because it's more demanding, it's more rewarding as well.

1. A leader is chosen by lot.
2. The dominoes are shuffled face-downwards. If there are two players, each player takes 7 dominoes. If there are three players, each player takes 6 dominoes. If there are four or five players, each player takes 5 dominoes. The remaining dominoes are left face-downwards and form the boneyard.

3. Play must begin with the player who has the double-6 in his hand placing it in the middle of the table. If none of the players has the 6/6, the leader draws a domino from the boneyard. If he draws the 6/6, he plays it. If he doesn't, the player on his left draws from the boneyard. If *he* gets the 6/6 he plays it. If he doesn't, the player on *his* left, draws from the boneyard. This goes on around the group, until one of the players has drawn the 6/6 – *providing* that 2 dominoes are left untouched in the boneyard at all times. If all but 2 of the dominoes in the boneyard have been drawn and no one has yet drawn the double-6, the game is abandoned, all the dominoes are reshuffled and play starts all over again.

4. Once the 6/6 has been played, the next player must play another 6 domino against either of the ends *or* either of the sides of the 6/6. If he cannot play and there are more than 2 dominoes left in the boneyard, he can draw one of them. If he still cannot play, he passes and it becomes the next player's turn.

5. This goes on around the group until four dominoes have been played against the 6/6, one joining each end and one joining either side. Once four dominoes have been played against the 6/6, four doubles must be played against each of the other ends of the four dominoes already played against the 6/6.

6. Play continues like this, with each arm waiting to have the same number of dominoes before a new layer can be started, until one of the players manages to get rid of all his dominoes. That player is the winner. However, if after a while, no one can play and the game is blocked, the winner is the player with the smallest number of pips on his dominoes.

If the question is, 'How do you make a Maltese cross?' the answer must be 'Tread on his toe!' But if what you really want to know is how to make the shape of a Maltese Cross, the answer is to play this ancient and amusing domino game. You will need four players and here are the rules:

1. When the dominoes have been shuffled face-downwards, each of the four players takes 7 dominoes.
2. The player who has drawn the double-6 begins by placing his 6/6 face-up in the middle of the table.
3. The next player, who is sitting on the first player's left, must now play a 6 domino but he can join it on to *either side* or *either end* of the first player's double-6.
4. The third player must now either play another 6 domino, joining it to the double-6, or play the

double of the non-6 end of the second player's domino. For example, if the second player had played a 6/1 and joined it to the top end of the double-6, the third player could *either* play another 6 domino (the 6/0, 6/2, 6/3, 6/4 or 6/5) against the bottom or either side of the double-6 *or* play the double-1 against the 1 end of the second player's 6/1. Doubles must always be played *across* the line of play.

5. The fourth player now has the alternative of playing another 6 domino *or* of playing the double-1 if the second player hasn't already done so *or* of joining a 1 domino to the double-1 if the second player has already played it.

6. The play moves round the group like this, with the two sides and the two ends of the first player's double-6 being joined by other 6 dominoes and with the other ends of those 6 dominoes being joined by the doubles of their suits. These other doubles must then have matching dominoes played against them and the doubles of their other ends must in turn be joined. With four lines radiating from the central double-6 and with every other piece having to be a double, played across the line, you finish the game with a shape that looks exactly like a Maltese Cross.

7. When a player is unable to play a domino on his turn, he passes. The first player to go out is the winner. If all the players pass in turn and no one can make a move, the game is blocked and the winner is then the player whose dominoes have the least number of pips on them.

Despite its romantic name, the glorious game of Matador has nothing to do with bullfighters and even less to do with bulls. It doesn't even come from sunny Spain, though, of course, thousands of Spaniards now play the game, just as hundreds of thousands of other people play it in different countries around the world. It's one of the oldest and most popular forms of dominoes and the rules are delightfully easy to learn.

1. The first player is chosen by lot.
2. All the players then draw their dominoes. If there are two players they take 7 pieces each; if three, 6; if four, 5.
3. The first player begins the line of play by placing any domino he likes on the table.
4. When the second player places his domino, it must, of course, match one of the ends of the first player's domino. It must do something else as well: *it must make the join total 7 pips*. To give you an example, let's suppose the first player had opened the game

with a simple 3/1, like this:

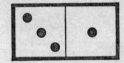

the second player has now got to play a domino that will either go at the 3-end or at the 1-end of the first player's domino and will make the join add up to 7. At the 1-end he can only put a 6, like this:

And at the 3-end he can only put a 4, like this:

This means that a 1 can only be joined by a 6, a 2 by a 5, a 3 by a 4, a 4 by a 3, a 5 by a 2 and a 6 by a 1.

5. The only thing is that all those 'only's' in the last rule weren't quite telling the truth – thanks to the Matadors, the four fantastic dominoes that can be played against any other domino (including a blank) without the join having to add up to 7. The Matadors are the three dominoes that total 7, the 6/1:

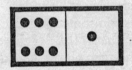

the 5/2:

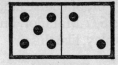

the 4/3:

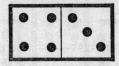

and the one domino that's a double-blank, the 0/0:

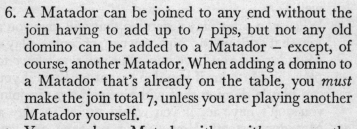

6. A Matador can be joined to any end without the join having to add up to 7 pips, but not any old domino can be added to a Matador – except, of course, another Matador. When adding a domino to a Matador that's already on the table, you *must* make the join total 7, unless you are playing another Matador yourself.

7. You can play a Matador either *with* or *across* the line of play. If you play the Matador with the line of play, you can join it to the line of play at either of its ends, as you please, but if a Matador is played across the line of play, the next domino joined to it must be played *with* the line of play. For example, if the 6/1 Matador has been played across the line of play like this:

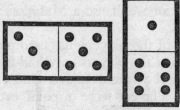

either a 6 or a 1 or, of course, another Matador can be joined to the 6/1 Matador, but it must be played with the line of play, like this:

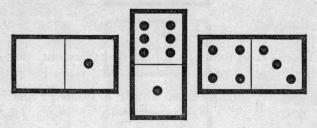

8. You can only play against the side – *not* the ends – of a Matador, and if you place any doubles across the line of play you can only play against their sides as well.

9. When you can't play a domino that will give you a join that adds up to 7 pips, you can, of course, play a Matador – if you have one – but you don't *have* to play the Matador if you don't want to. Even if you can play a domino that will give you a 7-pip join, you don't have to, if you would prefer to play a Matador instead. However, at no time are you obliged to play a Matador.

10. If you haven't got a domino that will make a 7-pip join, and you haven't got a Matador, or have a Matador but don't want to use it yet, you must draw a domino from the boneyard until you can make a join.

11. If the boneyard is empty, you can't make a join and don't have or won't use a Matador, you skip your turn.

12. When one of the players, has used up all his dominoes, or all of the players have had to pass a turn in succession, the round is over and the scores are added up. Players score 1 point every time they

make a join and every time they play a Matador. The player who manages to go out also gets 1 point for every pip in his opponents' hands. If no one has gone out when the round ends, each player gets 1 point for every pip in his opponents' and *minus* 1 point for every pip in his own hand.

13. You have as many rounds as necessary until one of the players scores 101 points. When you finish the round you are playing the player with the highest final total is declared the Matador champion.

If you've ever eaten a Chinese meal, you'll know that half an hour after you've finished it, you're ready to start eating all over again. It's just the same with Chinese Dominoes. Half an hour after you've finished a game, you're ready to start playing the game all over again. Of course, there is one vital difference between Chinese food and Chinese dominoes. You can go on and on and on playing the game and you won't get any fatter.

1. The aim of the game is to take *tricks* and be the player who ends up with the highest score.
2. The first player is chosen by lot.
3. When there are two players each player draws 7 dominoes from the shuffled set. When there are three players, each player draws 6 dominoes. When there are four players, each player draws 5 dominoes.
4. When all the players have taken and looked at their dominoes, the first player places any one of his dominoes face up on the table and immediately replaces it with another domino from the boneyard.
5. The second player now places any one of his dominoes alongside the first player's domino. He puts his face-upwards as well and then replaces it with another domino drawn from the boneyard.

6. Whenever a player places a domino on the table, he replaces it with another from the boneyard, until, of course, the boneyard is empty.
7. Now, to make a trick you must pair one of the dominoes in your hand with one of the dominoes at either end of the row of dominoes, so that the total number of pips on the domino in your hand and on one or other of the dominoes at the ends of the row comes to 12. This means, of course, that no tricks can be taken until there are at least 2 dominoes on the table. For example, if there were two dominoes placed side by side on the table and they were the 6/5 and the 4/2, you would be able to make a pair if it was your turn and you happened to have in your hand a 0/1 or a 6/0 or a 5/1 or a 3/3. You could pair your 0/1 with the 6/5 on the table and make 12 or pair either your 6/0 or your 5/1 or your 3/3 with the 4/2 on the table and still make 12. In short, if it's your turn and you can pair a domino from your hand with one of the end dominoes on the table and make the pips total 12, you have taken a trick. When a trick is taken, you take the 2 dominoes concerned off the table and put them in a discard pile. You also score 12 points.
8. You can also make a trick by matching one of the dominoes in your hand with *two* of the dominoes on the table so that the total number of pips on all three dominoes comes to 10, 20 or 30. This is *providing* that the two dominoes on the table are *either* the two end dominoes (that is to say that one of the dominoes is the first domino in the row and the other is the last) *or* the first two or the last two dominoes in the row (that is to say that one of them is the first domino and the other is the one right next to it or that one of them is the last domino and the other is

the last but one lying right alongside it.) If you take one of these three domino tricks, you will score 10 points if the total number of pips on the three dominoes is 10, 20 points if it's 20 and 30 points if it's 30.

9. Whenever a trick is taken, the dominoes involved are at once put on to the discard pile and not looked at again during the round.

10. Whenever a trick is taken, the score for that trick should be written down at once.

11. Whenever a trick is taken, the player who took that trick gets another turn immediately.

12. When a player runs out of dominoes, the round stops and the player who went out first is awarded the same number of points as there are pips on his opponents' dominoes. The number of points won by each player is now added up and the player with the highest total has won the round.

13. You play as many rounds as you can until you reach the round in which one of the player's scores tops the 1,000 mark. That's the last round. At the end of it, the player with the highest final total is declared the winner – and he celebrates his victory by taking everyone out for a delicious Chinese meal!

Muggins

Any muggins can play Muggins and almost every muggins does. It's one of the simplest games of dominoes for two, three or four players and certainly the best known. No one can call themselves a dab hand at dominoes until they've mastered Muggins, so if you don't know the rules of the game, start here.

1. The aim of the game is to get the highest possible score, and you score points when you place dominoes on the table so that the number of pips at the ends of the lines of play adds up to 5 and multiples of 5 (10, 15, 20 and so on) *and* by being the first player to have used up all your dominoes.

2. You score 1 point every time you make the number of pips at the ends of the lines of play add up to 5 or a multiple of 5 (which means you score 1 point for 5, 2 points for 10, 3 points for 15 and so on), and when you're the lucky one who goes out first you score 1 point for every 5 pips which remain in your opponents' hands at the moment when you made your last move. While the pips on the table must add up to 5 or a multiple of 5 exactly to count, the pips that remain in your opponents' hands when you go

41

out are rounded to the nearest 5. This means that 1 or 2 pips are worth nothing, 3, 4, 5, 6 or 7 pips are worth 1 point, 8, 9, 10, 11 or 12 pips are worth 2 points and so on.

3. You play as many hands as you like, until one of the players has scored 61 points. At the end of the hand during which the 61 point mark is passed, the player with the highest score is declared the winner.

4. Before beginning play, the dominoes are shuffled face-downwards and each player then picks his dominoes. With two players, each player takes 7 dominoes; with three, 6; with four, 5.

5. The player with the highest double plays first. If it happens to be a 5/5 then the first player actually scores 2 whole points in the opening move!

6. The players that follow must all join their dominoes to an open end in the line of play and must make sure the end of the domino they play matches the end in the line of play.

7. If a player has a playable domino, he *must* play it. If he hasn't he must draw dominoes from the bone-yard until he gets one. If the boneyard is empty, he must skip his turn until he *can* play.

8. Doubles must be played *across* the line of play, and the ends of a double are only open to play after the open side of the double has been played on.

9. When one of the players has used all the dominoes in his hand, that particular round is over, the score is totted up, the dominoes are reshuffled, fresh tea is brewed and a new round begins, with the opening move again going to the player with the highest double.

Five Up

Muggins is a game with a large and famous family of near- and not-so-near relations. Five Up is probably the closest of these. In fact, it's so close you could call it a twin. The two games are almost identical, but not quite. There are only three differences between the basic rules of Muggins and Five Up – and here they are:

1. The first player in Five Up is determined by lot and when he's been chosen he can begin by playing any domino in his hand.
2. The lead passes to the left with each new round of Five Up.
3. However many people are playing Five Up, each player begins with just five dominoes.

All Fives

If Muggins and Five Up are near-identical twins, then Muggins and Five Up and All Fives are almost-identical triplets. The rules for All Fives are the same as the rules for Muggins, with just five-all-important exceptions.

1. The first player is determined by lot and when he's been chosen he can begin by playing any domino in his hand.
2. The lead passes to the left with each new round.
3. However many people are playing, each player begins with just five dominoes.
4. Whenever a player makes a move that scores him a point and whenever a player plays a double, he is allowed an extra turn. If he hasn't a domino he can play in his extra turn, he must draw from the boneyard until he gets one, or until the boneyard is empty.
5. A player can't go out playing a domino that will give him a point or playing a double. If he plays a double or a domino that gives him a score and it's the last piece in his hand, he must draw from the boneyard until he has another move he can make or until the boneyard is empty. If the boneyard is already empty *before* he wants to play his last domino, he cannot play it. He skips his turn and play passes to the left as usual.

Seven-Toed Pete

Seven-toed Pete is one of
Muggins' American cousins.
To play the game you need
all the Muggins' rules with
five exceptions.

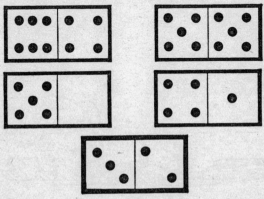

1. The lead player is chosen by lot.
2. The lead player must begin by placing on the table *either* a double *or* one of the scoring dominoes. With Seven-toed Pete, the five scoring dominoes are the ones whose pips total five or ten:

If the first player is unable to play a double or one of the scoring dominoes, play passes to the player on his left.

3. Whenever a player plays a double or plays a domino that earns him points, he gets another turn and he can carry on playing as long as he is able to – which, technically speaking, means that the first player could go out in his first move!

4. When a player plays his last domino, he must score with it if he can. If he is unable to score with it, the round is considered over and the hand score is totalled. However, if he can score with his last domino, the round continues, but he himself can't draw any more dominoes from the boneyard until his next turn.

5. The five scoring dominoes only score points in the game's first move. After that, they lose their magic power and become like all the other dominoes – only able to score when playing them makes the ends of the lines of play add up to 5 or multiples of 5.

Sniff

Sniff is one more member of the ever-growing Muggins' family and the rules for Sniff are exactly the same as the rules for Muggins, with just half-a-dozen important exceptions.

1. The lead player is chosen by lot.
2. The lead player can play any domino he chooses, but naturally if he begins by playing one of these, he scores with his opening move:

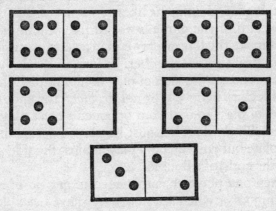

3. The first double played in the course of a round is called the Sniff and it can be played either *with* or *across* the line of play, as the player playing it chooses.
4. If the Sniff is played *across* the line of play, the open side must be played on before the ends can be played on.
5. If the Sniff is played *with* the line of play, the sides may be played on, but only *after* the open end has been played on.
6. All the doubles that are played after the Sniff *must* be played *across* the line of play.

Games from the Block family

Block

Block is the black-sheep of the Muggins' family. It's closely related to the great original all right, but some Muggins' fans feel that the differences between the two games stretch the bounds of family loyalty. All the same, the Muggins' rules apply to Block in general, with only a handful of particular differences. Here they are:

1. The lead player is chosen by lot and he can begin by playing any domino he likes.
2. The aim of the game is *not* to play a domino that will make the line of play end in a certain number or a multiple of that number. In fact, in Block the pips at the ends of the lines of play don't matter. The aim of Block is, believe it or not, to *block* the ends of the lines of play, so that your opponents *can't* play.
3. With Block, doubles must be played *across* the line of play, but you can only play against the side (never on the ends) of a double.
4. When one player has managed to get rid of all his dominoes or when all the players have been blocked so that no one can go out, the player with the fewest pips in his hand (if he went out, he'll have none) gets 1 point for every pip in his opponents' hands, minus 1 point for every pip in his own hand (if he has any).
5. You play as many rounds of Block as you like until you get to the round in which one player scores 101 or more points. That's the last round and the player with the highest score at the end of it wins the game.

Fours

Block, of course, is related to Muggins, but Block itself has a pretty impressive list of dependants and descendants. For a start, Fours is a member of the Block brood. *All* the Block rules apply to Fours, with three exceptions. And here they are:

1. Fours is a game for four players only and the four players can't form teams. They must play as four individuals.
2. The first player is chosen by lot.
3. A player can carry on playing so long as he can still make a match.

Sebastopol

You could say that Sebastopol was another chip off the old Block, because the two games are closely related. Just as it is important to master Muggins as soon as you begin to play with dominoes because so many other great games are based upon it, so must you brush up on the rules of Block for exactly the same reason. *All* the rules of Block apply to Sebastopol, with three exceptions.

1. If four people play, each player takes 7 dominoes and the player with the double-6 (6/6) leads. If three people play, the lead player is chosen by lot and each player takes 9 dominoes. Whoever gets the double-6 lays it on the table, and replaces it in his hand with the remaining domino in the boneyard. If the double-6 is the domino in the boneyard, it is simply played out at once. Either way, the lead player now plays to the double-6 and play passes, as usual, to the left.

2. The first four joins in the game must be to the double-6, like this:

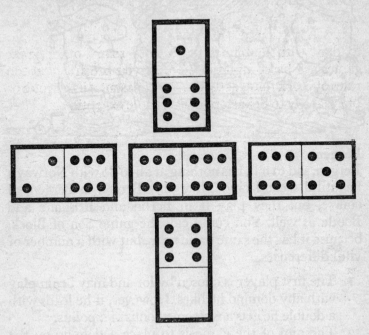

3. After the double-6, all the other doubles are played *with* the line of play, and only the open ends of doubles, not their sides can be played against. From here on the aim of the game and the methods of scoring are identical to those of Block.

Bergen

Bergen, sad to tell, has nothing at all to do with Norway's beautiful second city. They play Bergen in Bergen, of course, but they play it in Berlin and Brisbane and Bootle as well. You could call the game Son of Block, because it has the same basic rules, but with a number of vital differences.

1. The first player is chosen by lot and may begin play with any domino he likes. However, if he leads with a double he gets a welcome bonus of 2 points.

2. The aim of the game is to place a domino on the table so that when you have done so, the new ends of the line of play will match. For example, if there is a 6/1 at one end of the line and a 3/2 at the other, you will have to play a 2/6 at either end to make the ends of the line of play match. If you manage to make a match you score 2 points. You score 3 points if you make a match either playing with, or playing against, a double.

3. When a player goes out or all the players are blocked, the player with the most number of points in that round gets 1 extra point for each domino still in his opponents' hands, minus 1 point for each piece left in his own hand, if there are any.

Tiddly-Wink

Tiddly-Wink's the simplest of all Block's close relations. As a game it's got nothing to with being tiddly or with winking or even with the ancient sport of flicking plastic counters across the kitchen floor. It's simply another form of dominoes that's very like the game of Block. It's so like Block, in fact, that there is only one difference between the rules of the two games.

1. In Tiddly-Wink, *whenever* a player plays a double he is allowed to play a second domino if he wants and is able to do so. He doesn't have to take advantage of this privilege if he doesn't want to.

53

The French have given us so much more than frogs, snails and the *Marseillaise*. They've given us French Draw, a cheeky continental cousin of the *famille* Block. As you will expect, the basic Block rules apply, but there are some important differences.

1. The first player is chosen by lot.
2. With two or three players, they take 7 dominoes each. With four players, they take 6 dominoes each. The remaining dominoes form the boneyard.
3. The first player *must* choose a domino from his own hand and play it.
4. The next player can *either* match one of the ends of the first player's domino *or* choose to take as many dominoes as he likes from the boneyard – providing he leaves at least 2 dominoes in the boneyard – until he feels ready and able to play. He cannot say he is unable to play until he has taken all but 2 of the dominoes in the boneyard.
5. When the second player has either put a matching domino on the table or said he cannot play, it becomes the next player's turn. He does exactly the

same. This goes on around and around the group
with each player in his turn deciding whether to
play at once or draw, but always playing in the end,
when he can. At all times there must be at least 2
dominoes left in the boneyard.
6. The game ends either when one player manages to
get rid of all of his dominoes or when none of the
players can go. If one of the players manages to go
out first, that player is the winner. If none of the
players can go out, the pips on the dominoes remaining in the players' hands are counted and the
player with the lowest number of pips is declared
the winner.

Draw or Pass

French Pass and Draw or Pass are so alike they could be brother and sister, but like brother and sister, though they've an awful lot in common, they are still very different creatures. Draw or Pass is probably the more difficult of the two games.

1. The first player is chosen by lot.
2. With two or three players, they take 7 dominoes each. With four players, they take 6 dominoes each. The remaining dominoes form the boneyard.
3. The first player *must* choose a domino from his own hand and play it.
4. Now the second player can do one of *three* things. He can *either* match one of the ends of the first domino with a domino from his hand *or* he can choose to take as many dominoes as he likes from the boneyard (providing he leaves at least 2 there) *or* he can pass.
5. If a player chooses to draw a domino, or a number of dominoes, from the boneyard, he cannot play a domino in that turn too.
6. If he wants to pass, he can do so even if he has a matching domino in his hand.
7. When the second player has had his turn, the next player can either play a matching domino at once or draw from the boneyard or pass.
8. This goes on around and around the group, until all the players say 'Pass' in succession, when the game is over and the number of pips on the dominoes remaining in the players' hands is counted. The player with the lowest number of pips is the brilliant Draw or Pass champion.

Card Games for Dominoes

Elevens

Some of the best domino games are related to some of the best card games. Here is one for three or four players that's rather like a famous card game that's sometimes called Black Maria and sometimes called Bloody Mary. With Elevens the players take *tricks* according to *suits*, just as they do in Whist. Don't worry if you haven't the first idea what those terms mean and always thought 'tricks' were what you found at the Magic Circle and 'suits' were things that came from Moss Bros. Once you've read the rules through a couple of times, all will be clear.

1. The aim of the game is to keep your score as *low* as possible. You can do this *either* by taking as few of the scoring dominoes as possible *or* by taking all the scoring dominoes.
2. The scoring dominoes are the double-blank (0/0),

which scores 4 points, and the seven dominoes in the 3-suit (3/0, 3/1, 3/2, 3/3, 3/4, 3/5, 3/6), which each score 1 point:

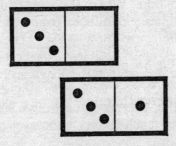

57

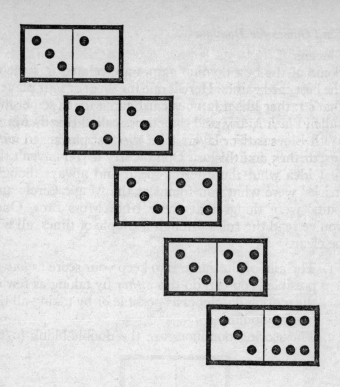

3. The first player is chosen by lot, and when there are three players each player plays as an individual, but when there are four players the players can play as two teams, with each player partnering the player opposite him. When there are four players each player takes 7 dominoes from the shuffled set. But when there are three players each player takes 9 dominoes, which will leave one left over in the bone-yard, to be collected by whoever takes the first trick.

4. When the players have drawn and studied their dominoes, each player chooses 3 of his pieces and

passes them, face-downwards, to the player sitting on his left. You cannot look at the dominoes that are being passed to you, until you have passed on the 3 dominoes you are getting rid of.

5. The first player, who is called the lead player, begins by playing any piece he chooses, declaring its suit as he does so. For example, if the first player led with the 4/5, like this:

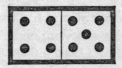

he could say the suit was 4 *or* 5. But if he began with a double, like this:

he could declare that the suit was 5 *or doubles*.

6. If they can, the players must follow the declared suit. So if the lead player has put a 4/5 on the table and declared the 5-suit and you are the next player and you have a domino with a 5 on it, you *must* play that domino. If you haven't got a 5, then, of course, you can put any domino you like down on the table.

7. When each of the players has placed a domino on the table, the three of four dominoes played are called a *trick*, and the trick is taken by the player who played the highest domino in the suit that led.

The double of a suit is the highest domino in the suit (5/5 in the case of the 5-suit), followed by numbers of the suit in descending order from 6 to blank (5/6, 5/4, 5/3, 5/2, 5/1, 5/0 in the case of the 5-suit).

8. The player who takes the trick, puts the dominoes he's taken by him face-downwards and no one can look at them again until the end of the round. In a three-handed game, the left-over domino is taken by the taker of the first trick and also put face-downwards by him.

9. The taker of a trick always has the lead for the next trick and can play any domino he likes.

10. After 7 tricks have been taken (in a four-handed game) or after 9 tricks have been taken (in a three-handed game), the scores are tallied. If a player has taken *all* the scoring dominoes with his tricks, each of his opponents is given 22 points. In the case of a four-handed game, when the players have divided into two teams, the two players in a team only have to have collected all the scoring dominoes between them for their opponents to be awarded 22 points each.

11. If no one player or no single team has collected all the scoring dominoes, then the individual players or individual teams are each awarded points according to the scoring dominoes they were lucky enough to take with their tricks.

12. At the end of each round of 7 or 9 tricks, the player with the highest score – that's to say the poor fellow with the *worst* score – is allowed to be the lead player for the next round. If he doesn't choose to lead, he can pass the lead to the player on his left, who, under the circumstances, *must* lead.

13. You go on playing any number of rounds of Elevens, until you get to the round in which one of the

players' scores tops the 101 mark. That's the last round and whichever player – of whichever team – has the lowest score at the end of that round is victorious.

Twenty-ones
Here's a form of dominoes that's got nothing to do with that delightfully dangerous gambling game called Twenty-one. It's as much fun, less expensive and a close cousin of that other domino delight, Elevens (which, of course, has got nothing to do with mid-morning snacks and cups of tea and coffee). In fact, the rules for Elevens and Twenty-ones are identical, but the scoring is significantly different.

1. With Twenty-ones, the scoring dominoes do *not* include the seven pieces of the 3-suit. Instead they consist of the ten dominoes that feature 5 or 6 or 7 pips:

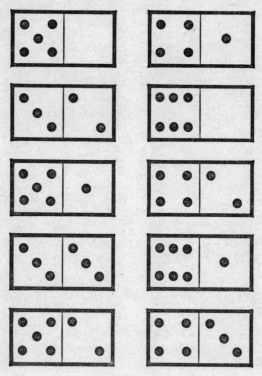

With Twenty-ones, these ten dominoes all score 1 point each. The double-blank, however, scores rather more:

   With Elevens, the double-blank costs a mere 4 points. With Twenty-ones the double-blank scores a frightening 11 points!

2. If you or your team manage to collect all the scoring points in your tricks, your opponents will still only be awarded 22 points each.

3. With Twenty-ones, the last round is the one in which one of players' scores tops the 210 mark.

Forty-twos

If Elevens and Twenty-ones are a little like Black Maria or Bloody Mary, Forty-twos is a lot like Bridge, one of the most difficult, dangerous and delightful of all card games. The real difference between Forty-twos and Bridge is that you play Bridge with cards and Forty-twos with dominoes, but apart from that, they've got a lot in common, including a great deal of talk about *tricks* and *suits* and *bids*. Both games are hard to master, so study the rules of Forty-twos with care. You will probably need to read them twice or more before you can be certain of becoming world champion.

1. Forty-twos is a game for four players, playing in two teams. Each player sits opposite his partner. Like Elevens and Twenty-ones, it's a game where players take tricks in suits. Unlike Elevens and Twenty-ones, it is also a game where players can *bid* – that is, before starting to play they say how many points they expect to make in that round.

2. In each round the maximum number of points available is 42 (which is why the game isn't called Seventeens or Five Hundreds). Each trick that is taken brings 1 point with it to the team that takes it and in each round there are, of course, 7 tricks to be taken. In Forty-twos there are also five special dominoes, known as the *honours* and, if you manage to win one of them in a trick, you get a bonus of either 5 or 10 points. Here are the three 5-point honours dominoes. Take any one of them and you score 5 points (10 if you take two, of course, and 15 if you take three):

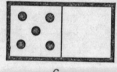

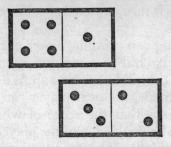

And here are the two 10 points honours dominoes. Take either of these and you get a bonus of 10 points – take both and it's a bonus of 20:

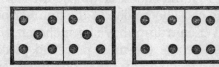

3. The first bidder is chosen by lot. When he has been chosen, all the players take seven dominoes from the shuffled set.

4. When everyone has had a chance to look at their dominoes, the first bidder makes his bid – that's to say he declares how many points he and his partner expect to collect between them in that round. He must start the bidding at 30 points or more, but he can't start it at less. If he decides he doesn't want to bid, he simply says 'No bid' and the player on his left is allowed to make the opening bid. If he decides not to, the chance to bid passes to the player on his left, and so on around the group. If no one bids, the dominoes are collected, reshuffled and a new hand is drawn.

5. When the first bid has been made, the player sitting on the left of the first bidder can now make a bid of his own, providing his bid is higher than the first bidder's. The third and fourth players can bid as

well, in their turn, or decide against bidding, as they please.

6. The bidding can continue *either* until three players have said 'No bid' in succession *or* until 42 has been bid, when the bidding must stop. When the bid of 42 has been made, the next player can say 'Doubled', which means that the score of whoever wins the round will be doubled, and the player after that can say 'Redoubled', which means the score of whoever wins the round is quadrupled!

7. When the bidding is completed, the player who made the first bid chooses trumps for the round. For trumps he can choose one of the number of suits or doubles. When trumps have been chosen, the trump dominoes become the most powerful pieces in the game and can take any other dominoes, except, of course, other trump dominoes of a higher value. If a number suit is trumps, say the 4-suit, the double of that suit is the strongest piece (4/4), followed by the other dominoes in the suit in descending order (4/6, 4/5, 4/3, 4/2, 4/1, 4/0). If doubles are trumps, the double-6 is the most powerful piece, followed by the other doubles in descending order (6/6, 5/5, 4/4, 3/3, 2/2, 1/1, 0/0).

8. The first bidder can also declare *No trumps* if he chooses. When he declares 'No trumps', the higher of the two numbers on the domino he first plays becomes trumps for that round, and the double of that number will be the strongest trump, followed by the remaining dominoes in that suit in descending order.

9. Whatever is trumps, the players must follow suit when they can. When they can't, they are allowed to play any domino they like.

10. When the first bidder has chosen trumps, he plays

his first domino and, unless he declared 'No trumps', this first domino *must* be a trump.

11. Whoever plays the highest trump will take the first trick. He then plays the first domino for the second trick. It needn't be a trump this time. The players must again follow suit if they can, but if they can't, they may play any other suit they fancy, including, of course, a trump. The trick will be won by whoever played the highest domino of the suit of the first domino *or*, if a trump was played, by whoever played the highest trump domino.

12. When a player takes a trick, he keeps the four dominoes in that trick right by him. After he has studied them, he must keep them face-downwards until the end of the round.

13. When all 7 tricks have been won, the round is over and the scores are calculated. If the player who made the highest bid and his partner score enough points to at least reach their bid, they then get 1 point for each of the tricks they have taken between them, plus any of the 5- or 10-point honours they have won by taking tricks including the honours dominoes. The opponents also score 1 point for each of their tricks, together with any points from any honours dominoes they have managed to secure. However, if the player who made the highest bid and his partner *fail* to score enough points to reach their bid, they score nothing and their opponents get both the number of points in the bid *and* any points they have earned by taking tricks and honours themselves.

14. At the end of each round, the dominoes are reshuffled and the game starts all over again, with the opening bid passing to the left with each round.

15. The rounds continue until one team scores 250 or more. At the end of the round in which the 250 mark is passed, the team with the highest final total is declared the overall winner.

Bingo

Forty-twos may be a lot like Bridge, but Bingo is nothing like Bingo – either Bingo the game or Bingo the dog or even *Bingo* the strange play about William Shakespeare by a strange playwright called Edward Bond. If Bingo, the domino game, is like anything at all it's like a Victorian card game called Sixty-six. Here are the rules, so you can see for yourself.

1. Bingo is a rare thing in domino games: it's for only two players.
2. The first player is chosen by lot.
3. The dominoes are shuffled and each player takes 7, leaving 14 face-downwards in the boneyard.
4. The second player begins by turning up one of the 14 dominoes in the boneyard so that it's lying face-upwards. He leaves it there and the first player chooses one end of this exposed domino to be trumps. For example, if the second player turns up a 3/4, the first player can choose the 3-suit or the 4-suit as trumps. However, if the second player turns up a double (say 3/3), the first player has no alternative when it comes to choosing trumps (3 in this example).
5. The first player now places a piece from his hand on to the table. It can be any piece he likes. The second player follows and places a domino from his hand on to the table.
6. If the domino played by the second player matches either end of the domino played by the first player, the trick is taken by the player with the higher other end. For example, if the first player played a 3/4 and the second player played a 3/6 the second player would take the trick. However if the first player had played a 3/4 and the second player had

69

played a 3/1 the first player would have taken the trick. At least, that's what happens normally. It doesn't happen, however, if either player has played a trump domino or the Bingo domino. A trump always takes a non-trump and a higher trump always takes a lower trump. The Bingo takes everything! In Bingo, the Bingo domino is the most powerful piece in the game and this is what it looks like:

7. Of course, if the domino played by the second player does *not* match either end of the domino played by the first player, the first player takes the trick – *unless* the second player has played a trump or the Bingo domino, in which case the second player takes the trick.
8. Whoever takes the trick, gathers the two taken dominoes near him and leaves them face-down until the end of the game.
9. Whoever takes the trick also has the lead for the next trick, but before the lead is played, both players draw one new domino each from the boneyard, as long as there are dominoes left there.
10. For the last draw from the boneyard, the second player has to take the domino he turned face-upwards right at the beginning of the game. From this point onward, the second player can no longer play *any* piece he chooses. He must now match one end of the lead domino *or* play a trump *or* play the Bingo domino every time if he possibly can. Only if

he really doesn't have a matching domino, a trump or the Bingo, can he play any other domino of his choice.

11. The scoring doesn't come until the end of the game when all fourteen tricks have been taken, but it is possible to earn some bonus points along the way. Whenever the player whose lead it is leads a double (the 5/5, for example) and at the same time shows his opponent that he still has another double in his hand (the 2/2, for example), he gets a bonus of 3 points *if* he also takes the trick. If he has led one double, revealed another in his hand, and then lost the trick in question, he gets nothing. If you like, you can go on doing this at every turn, providing you have enough doubles to lead, because you can reveal the same double in your own hand each time.

12. After the fourteen tricks have been played and taken, the round is over and the two players can work out how many points they have scored. They look at the dominoes they have taken and do their sums:

The Bingo domino scores 14 points.
The double of trumps scores the same number of points as there are pips on the domino.
All the other doubles score 3 points each.
All the trumps (except the double) score the same number of points as there are pips on the other, non-trump end of the piece.
The remaining dominoes score nothing.

13. You have as many games as you can until one of the players reaches a score of 66 points. At the end of that round, the player with the higher score has won the game.

Pontoon

Twenty-ones may not have been anything like the card game called Twenty-one, but Pontoon is. It's an exciting gambling game for three or more domino players, so you will need plenty of nerve as well as lots of money if you are going to enjoy Pontoon. You can play the game with pounds, pennies, buttons, shells or milk-bottle tops, but remember, Pontoon is a game of chance more than skill, so you must expect bad luck as well as good luck and don't gamble your life-savings away!

1. One player is chosen by lot to be the Banker. All the other players are simply 'players'. With each round the Bank moves to the left, so everyone gets a chance to be Banker several times in a game.
2. The dominoes are shuffled face-downwards and all the players, including the Banker, draw two dominoes.
3. Each player is playing as an individual against the Bank, the aim of the game being to get a better hand than the Banker gets, the perfect hand being one of exactly 21 points. If you get 22 or more points, you've lost. If you get fewer points than the Banker, you've lost. If you get exactly the same as the Banker, you've also lost – with one exception, which we'll come to later.

72

4. The first thing to learn with Pontoon is the value of the dominoes. Obviously, each domino is worth its face value:

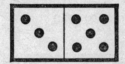

the 3/5 is worth 8 points, the double-blank (0/0) is worth 0 points, the 1/3 is worth 4 points, the double-6 (6/6) is worth 12 points and so on.

5. That's not all. The seven dominoes that include a blank (the 0/0, 0/1, 0/2, 0/3, 0/4, 0/5, 0/6) have *alternative values* as well. A blank can be considered *either* as being worth 0 points *or* as being worth 7 points, according to the wishes of the player holding the domino in question.

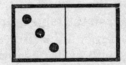

This means, for example, that the 0/3 can be worth either 3 points or 10 points, according to the wishes of the player holding the piece.

6. What's more, the six doubles apart from the double-blank (the 1/1, 2/2, 3/3, 4/4, 5/5, 6/6) also have *alternative values*. A double can be considered *either* as being worth its face value *or* as being worth half its face value, again according to the wishes of the player holding the domino in question.

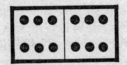

This means, for example, that the double-6 (6/6) can be worth either 12 points or simply 6 points, according to the wishes of the player holding the piece.

7. Combine Rules 5 and 6 and you will realize that the double-blank (0/0) can be a very useful piece indeed:

In Pontoon, the double-blank can be worth either 0 points *or* 7 points *or* 14 points, according to the wishes of the happy player holding the piece.

8. When all the players have drawn 2 dominoes, all the players excepting the Banker, must place a bet of 2p (that's 1p for each domino). This they do by placing the 2p (the £2, the 2 buttons, the 2 shells or the 2 milk-bottle tops) on the table in front of them.

9. Now play moves round the table, starting on the left of the Banker, with each player saying whether he will *stick* or *draw*. If a player decides to stick it means that he doesn't want any more dominoes because he feels that he is near enough to the magic figure of 21 points and another domino may push him over the mark. When a player has said 'Stick', he does nothing, but waits quietly for the end of the round.

10. If a player decides to draw it means that he wants more dominoes to bring his number of points nearer to 21. He must add another 1p to his bet when he says 'Draw' and simply draw one of the dominoes from the boneyard. When he has got his 3 dominoes, he can either day 'Draw' again, add another 1p to his bet and draw a fourth domino, or say 'Stick' and

sit quietly until the end of the round. He can go on saying 'Draw' as many times as he likes, providing he adds 1p to his bet for each domino he draws and providing he doesn't go over 21 points in doing so.

11. When a player says 'Draw' and takes another domino and that domino pushes his total score over 21 points he says 'Bust' rather sadly and gives his bet to the Banker – who grins! Once a player has said 'Bust' he is out of the game for that round.

12. When all the players have decided to stick or have gone bust in the process, it's the Banker's turn to play. He now reveals his two dominoes and decides whether or not to stick with them as they are or draw one or more dominoes. Since the Banker doesn't place any bets himself, he doesn't have to pay for any of the dominoes he draws. If the Banker goes bust by getting more than 21 points, he has to pay all the players who haven't gone bust as well, according to the rates described in rule 14.

13. Whatever the Banker scores, whether it's 14, 17, 19 or 21 points, he only pays those players who haven't gone bust and who have scored *more* than him. If a player ties with the Banker, the player loses, *unless* the player has a score of exactly 21 points made up of 3 dominoes, of which one must be the double-blank. In that case, the Banker pays the player, even if the Banker also has 21 points.

14. The Banker wins when he scores the same as, or more than, a player without going bust, with the one exception mentioned in the last rule, and when the Banker beats a player he simply takes the player's bet. A player wins whenever he scores more than the Banker without going bust and whenever he scores 21 points with just three dominoes, including the double-blank. Here is what the Banker

must pay a player who beats him:

A 2p bet costs the Banker 4p.

A 3p bet costs the Banker 9p.

A 4p bet costs the Banker 16p.

A 5p bet costs the Banker 25p.

A 6p bet costs the Banker 36p.

A 7p bet costs the Banker 49p.

An 8p bet costs the Banker 64p.

A 9p bet costs the Banker 81p.

It's never possible to place a bet of more than 9p because it's never possible to draw more than 9 dominoes without going bust. In fact, there are only four ways of placing a 9p bet and successfully scoring 21 points – and, according to one American domino demon who has fed all the figures into a high-powered computer, the chances of your getting one of those four ways are 1 in 627,979,968,000 – so don't bank on it!

15. When the Banker has payed the other players or the other players have paid the Banker, as the case may be, all the dominoes are gathered together and reshuffled ready for the next round. For the second round, the player who was on the left of the Banker for the first round becomes the new Banker.

16. Before playing Pontoon, it is probably a good idea to make sure that every player starts with the same amount of money – say 20p, or 30 buttons, or 40 milk-bottle tops, or 50 Smarties. When a player has lost all his money, or is reduced to 1p, he is declared *bankrupt* and must leave the game.

17. A game of Pontoon can have any number of rounds. It can either last until all the players are bored with it or last until all but one player is bankrupt. That one player will be the winner – and will have all the other players' money to prove it!

Concentration

If you've ever spent an afternoon playing Pelmanism, an infuriating card game that shows you what a terrible memory you've got, you are certain to enjoy Concentration. It's an exciting domino game for any number of players that simply calls – surprise! surprise! – for lots and lots of *concentration*.

1. The aim of the game is to take tricks, and as many of them as possible, but the tricks in Concentration aren't quite like the tricks in any other domino game. With Concentration, a trick is any pair of dominoes whose total value comes to 12. For example, to make a trick with a double-6 (6/6), you've got to pair it with a double-blank (0/0):

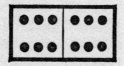 

77

and to make a trick with the 6/5, you've got to pair it with the 1/0:

 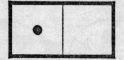

There are 34 different ways in which the 28 dominoes can be paired to make the game's 14 tricks.

2. Before play begins, all the dominoes are shuffled and placed flat on the table face-downwards.

3. The first player is chosen by lot and his move consists of picking up any two of the dominoes on the table and turning them face-upwards. If the total number of pips on the two exposed dominoes comes to 12, the player takes the trick, takes the two dominoes off the board, puts them by him and gets another turn. However, if the player chooses two dominoes whose pips do *not* total 12, he replaces the dominoes face-downwards on the table and it is now the turn of the next player.

4. As usual, play passes to the left, and when all the tricks have been taken and there are no more dominoes left on the table, the scores are added up. Players score 1 point for every trick they take and the player with the highest score is the winner of the round. After ten rounds, the player with the highest score is the over-all champion.

Domino Patience

This is the standard game of Domino Patience. It isn't all that thrilling, but it's quite easy to learn and quite fun to play.

1. Shuffle the dominoes face-downwards and draw 5.
2. Look at your dominoes and play one of them by placing it in the middle of the table.
3. Now match either end of your first domino with another domino from your hand. Now another. And another.
3. Whenever you find you haven't got a domino in your hand to match either end of the line of play on the table, draw a new domino from the boneyard.
5. If you manage to get rid of all the dominoes in your hand, congratulations, you've won! If you've drawn all the dominoes from the boneyard and you're still blocked, bad luck, you've lost! Better luck next time.

Domino Dozen

There are several games of domino solitaire like this one. It's a very enjoyable game, but a very frustrating one too, because almost every time you think you're just about to win, something goes wrong – and you lose! When you've had a chance to look at the rules, see how well (or how badly!) you do.

1. Shuffle the dominoes face-downwards and draw 6 of them.
2. Line the 6 dominoes in a row, face-upwards and side by side.
3. If in your row of 6 dominoes there are any two dominoes which between them have a total of 12 pips, you can discard those 2 dominoes. For example, if your row of 6 dominoes includes the double-6 and the double-blank you can discard them at once. When you discard the dominoes you simply take them away from the row and place them in a discard pile.
4. Each time you discard 2 dominoes, because the number of pips on the pair of them adds up to 12, you replace the 2 discarded dominoes with 2 new dominoes from the boneyard.
5. If you are able to discard all 28 dominoes in the set, you've won! If you are not able to discard them all, you've lost.

Five Columns

If you find Domino Dozen tricky, you'll find Five Columns almost impossible! It's a game you *can* and *will* win, but don't expect to win it the first time or the second time, or even the third time you play. Unless you are a very lucky sort of person (and let's hope you are), you will have to play Five Columns a lot before you start to win the game regularly.

1. Shuffle the dominoes face-downwards and draw 3 to place at one side of the table.
2. Leave the remaining 25 dominoes face-downwards and lay them out horizontally in 5 columns with 5 dominoes in each column.
3. Now turn all 25 dominoes over, but leave them face-upwards in exactly the same position.
4. Look at the 5 dominoes at the bottoms of the 5 columns. If the pips on any 2 of those 5 bottom dominoes add up to 12, remove those 2 dominoes and place them in the discard pile.
5. Now look at the 5 columns again and see if you can discard another 2 of the bottom 5 dominoes. And another 2. And another 2.
6. Don't forget to keep an eye on the 3 dominoes you put aside in Rule 1, because you are allowed at any point in the game to match any one of them with any one of the 5 dominoes at the bottom of the 5

columns and discard the pair if their pips total 12.

7. When a column has been completely discarded, the bottom domino from another column can be moved into its place.

8. When you manage to discard all 28 dominoes, you win! When you don't, you don't!

Seven Towers

If Five Columns seems almost impossible, Seven Towers will seem *totally* impossible! It's called a game of patience and patience is certainly what it calls for. If you win one game out of ten, you're doing well. If you win more games than you lose, you're some kind of genius. If you win just once in a lifetime, you're normal!

1. Shuffle the dominoes face-downwards, draw 7 and lay them face-downwards in a row.
2. Draw another 7 dominoes and lay them face-downwards on top of the first 7.
3. Draw 7 more dominoes and lay them face downwards on top of the last 7.
4. Draw 7 more dominoes and lay them face-*upwards* on top of the last 7 dominoes. You should now have 7 small towers made of 4 dominoes each.
5. Look carefully at the 7 top dominoes. If the combined number of pips on any 2 of them comes to 12, you can discard those 2 dominoes. Take them off their piles and put them into a discard pile.
6. Whenever you discard 2 dominoes, turn up the 2 dominoes underneath. Look again at the tops of the 7 towers and see if there are any more pairs that add up to 12. If there are, discard them and turn up the dominoes underneath.
7. When all the dominoes in one of the towers have been discarded, you may *not* move any other domino into the empty space.
8. If you manage to discard all 28 dominoes in this way, you're a champion. If you don't manage to do it, don't worry: you're simply human.

No one quite knows how this entertaining game of solitaire got its name, but it's probably from that famous
rhyme:

> Patience is a virtue,
> Virtue is a grace,
> Grace is a naughty girl
> Who wouldn't wash her face!

Whatever you happen to be called, if patience happens
to be one of your virtues this is a domino game that you
will enjoy playing on your own.

1. Shuffle the dominoes and lay all 28 of them face-
   downwards in a straight line.
2. Now turn all of them over so that they are face-up,
   making sure that you turn each one over in the same
   way.
3. Now look carefully at the row of 28 dominoes. If
   there are any 2 dominoes on which the adjoining
   pips are alike horizontally you can discard them.
   For example if the 6/5 is right next to the 6/0 so

that the 6 ends of the dominoes are side by side, you can discard both of them at once.

4. Whenever 2 dominoes are discarded, you push the remaining dominoes together so that you keep a straight line of touching dominoes at all times.

5. You win the game if you manage to discard all 28 dominoes, but be warned: you won't win very often!

One Pip Less

Here's a solitaire game that you'll win if you're lucky, but you'll lose if you're not. Skill doesn't really enter into this game. Luck is what you need – and lots of it.

1. Shuffle the dominoes face-downwards and draw 4.
2. Lay the 4 dominoes side by side and face-up. Add up the number of pips on each domino and if any one domino has one pip less on it than any other domino, you can discard that domino. For example if your 4 dominoes happen to be the 6/6, the 3/1, the 2/1 and the 4/5, you can discard the 2/1 because it's got one pip less than the 3/1.
3. When you have looked at the 4 first dominoes and, if possible, discarded any domino that has one pip less than any other domino, you must draw 4 more dominoes from the boneyard and lay them face-up on top of the first 4 dominoes. (Of course, if you have already discarded one or more of the original 4 dominoes, you will lay the new dominoes on top of the spaces left by the discarded dominoes.)
4. You now add up the number of pips on each of the new top dominoes and if any domino has one pip less than any other domino you remove it. When you have discarded what dominoes you can, you put a further 4 dominoes on top of the old piles. You keep doing this until you have laid out all 28 dominoes.
5. If you manage to end up with just the double-6, having discarded all 27 of the other dominoes in the set, you're the winner. Well done!

Double Trouble

This isn't a game of solitaire to try when you are lying in bed recovering from 'flu, the measles or a major operation. To play Double Trouble, you need to be in peak condition, so if you're a weedy weakling you'd better go back to Domino Patience right away. However, if you're fit as a fiddle, read on.

1. Shuffle the dominoes face-down, draw 7 and lay them face-downwards in a row. Now do just as you did in Seven Towers, and lay 7 more on top of the first 7, and 7 more on top of the second 7, and then the last 7 on top of that, making sure that the last 7 are turned face-upwards.
2. The aim of the game is to end up with 7 columns with one double domino at the bottom of each column and all four dominoes in each column being of the same suit. For example, if at the bottom of column 1 you manage to get the double-5, then the 3 other dominoes on top of the 5/5 must also be of the 5 suit (the 5/0, the 5/2 and the 5/6, say).
3. Now, you can only shift a domino from the top of one column to the top of another if one of its

numbers matches one of the numbers on the domino which it's about to cover. At no time can you have more than 5 dominoes in any one column.

4. Whenever you shift a domino and reveal a face-down domino underneath it, you can turn the face-down domino face-up.

5. You can never, of course, have more than 7 columns, but if you shift all four dominoes away from one column, you can shift a domino from the top of one of the other columns into the empty space *providing* the domino you are shifting is a double.

6. When you have finished, the 7 doubles can be in any order in the line, providing that there is one at the bottom of every column and the three dominoes above each of the doubles can be any dominoes, providing their suits match the suits of the doubles beneath them. If you can achieve this, you have won.

Chance Solitaire

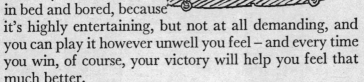

This game
of domino solitaire
is great fun because it
is purely and simply a
game of chance. It's an
ideal way of passing
time if you're ill and
in bed and bored, because
it's highly entertaining, but not at all demanding, and
you can play it however unwell you feel – and every time
you win, of course, your victory will help you feel that
much better.

1. Shuffle the dominoes and lay all 28 of them in a straight line face-downwards.
3. Starting at the left-hand end of the row, begin counting from 0 to 12 and every time you speak a number touch a domino. If you happen to be touching the number as you call it (you've got your finger on the double-blank as you begin, or you reach 6/5 as you get to 11), you can discard the domino in question.
4. When you get to the end of the line, go back to the beginning again and keep counting.
5. You go on counting from 0 to 12 over and over again, going along the row from left to right, *either* until you have discarded all the dominoes – in which case you're a winner – or until you can't get rid of any more of the dominoes – in which case you're a loser. Bad luck. Have another go.

DOMINO PUZZLES

1. First Square

Here's a puzzle you shouldn't have to puzzle over for too long. Take the 6 lowest dominoes in the set – the 0/0, the 0/1, the 0/2, the 1/1, the 1/2 and the 2/2 – and arrange them in a square so that all the joins match in number. The shape of the square should be just like this one:

You will find the solution to this and all the other puzzles at the end of this chapter.

2. Second Square

Take the same 6 dominoes as you used for the First Square – the 0/0, the 0/1, the 0/2, the 1/1, the 1/2 and the 2/2 – and arrange them in exactly the same-shaped square, but this time do it so that each of the four sides of the square contains the same number of pips.

3. Triangular Trouble

For this puzzle you will need the same 6 dominoes as you used for the first two – that's to say the 0/0, the 0/1, the 0/2, the 1/1, the 1/2 and the 2/2. Arrange the 6 dominoes to form an equilateral triangle that looks like this:

The puzzling part is that you have to make sure that each of the three sides of the triangle contains exactly the same number of pips, but at the same time you must make sure that none of the joins match.

4. First Rectangle

Since we've had a couple of square problems and a triangular one, it's probably about time we had a rectangular puzzle. For this one you'll need the same 6 dominoes – the 0/0, the 0/1, the 0/2, the 1/1, the 1/2, the 2/2 – and the same quick-wittedness you've used before. You have got to use the dominoes to create a rectangle that looks exactly like this:

The puzzling part of the problem comes in making sure that each of the four sides of the rectangle contains precisely the same number of pips.

5. Giant Square

Here's the shape you've got to create for this puzzle:

You can use the 10 lowest dominoes in the set – that's to say the 0/0, the 0/1, the 0/2, the 0/3, the 1/1, the 1/2, the 1/3, the 2/2, the 2/3 and the 3/3 – but you must make sure that the number of pips on each of the four sides of the Giant Square is the same and that none of the joins match.

6. The Three Rectangles

Take the 15 lowest dominoes in the set (the 0/0, the 0/1, the 0/2, the 0/3, the 0/4, the 1/1, the 1/2, the 1/3, the 1/4, the 2/2, the 2/3, the 2/4, the 3/3, the 3/4, the 4/4) and form 3 separate rectangles with them, so that all the joins are matching. Each of the rectangles should look like this:

7. The Five Lines

With the same 15 dominoes you used to make the Three Rectangles, form 5 lines, with 3 dominoes in each line, like this:

In each of the 5 lines the joins must match and there must be exactly the same number of pips in each line.

8. The Seven Lines

Take a complete set of dominoes and discard all the
pieces in the 6-suit. You are now left with 21 dominoes.
Arrange the 21 dominoes in seven lines with 3 dominoes
in each line, so that each line contains exactly the same
number of pips and all the joins match.

9. Three More Rectangles

Using the same 21 dominoes, form three rectangles.
Each rectangle should contain 7 dominoes and should
look like this:

The problem is to make sure that all twelve sides – that's
to say each of the four sides on each of the three triangles
– contain exactly the same number of pips. It's the
trickiest puzzle you've had to tackle so far, but keep
trying and you should succeed.

10. The Seven Squares

Take all 28 dominoes and make them into seven squares, with each square formed like this:

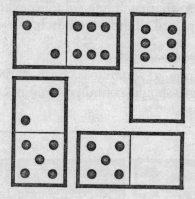

All the joins in each of the seven squares must match, but to make life even more difficult for you, you *can't* use the example we've just given you as one of the actual squares.

11. The Two Lines

Using the 6 lowest dominoes in the set – our old friends
the 0/0, the 0/1, the 0/2, the 1/1, the 1/2 and the 2/2
– form two lines, with three pieces in each line:

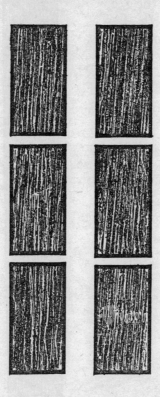

Each line must contain the same number of pips and
each of the joins must match.

12. The Two Columns

Take the 10 lowest dominoes
in the set – the 0/0, the 0/1,
the 0/2, the 0/3, the 1/1,
the 1/2, the 1/3, the 2/2,
the 2/3 and the 3/3 –
and arrange them in two
columns like this:

All the joins must match and
you must end with a total
of 15 pips in each column.

13. The Two Rectangles

Take the same 10 dominoes you used to build the Two Columns and turn them into two rectangles, looking like this:

Each of the eight sides (that's to say all four sides on both rectangles) must contain exactly the same number of pips and, for once, it doesn't matter whether or not the joins match.

14. Another Three Rectangles

With the lowest 15 dominoes in the set – the 0/0, the 0/1, the 0/2, the 0/3, the 0/4, the 1/1, the 1/2, the 1/3, the 1/4, the 2/2, the 2/3, the 2/4, the 3/3, the 3/4 and the 4/4 – form three rectangles looking like this one:

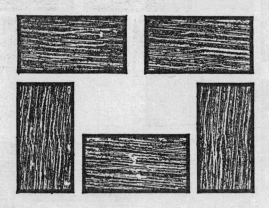

Each of the twelve sides (that means all four sides of each of the three rectangles) must contain exactly the same number of pips, but there is no need for the joins to match.

15. The Three Columns

Discard the 7 dominoes of the 6-suit and use the remaining 21 dominoes to build three columns, with 7 dominoes in each column. Each of the columns must contain exactly the same number of pips and the joins must all match.

16. The Giant Eight

Take the 10 lowest dominoes in the set – the 0/0, the 0/1, the 0/2, the 0/3, the 1/1, the 1/2, the 1/3, the 2/2, the 2/3 and the 3/3 – and arrange them to form a rather square figure of eight, like this:

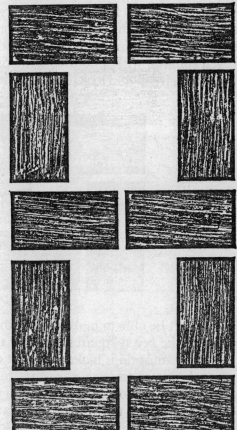

Both the vertical columns (that's to say the two sides of the figure) and the three horizontal rows (that's to say the 2 dominoes at the top of the figure, the 2 in the middle and the 2 at the bottom), must contain exactly the same number of pips.

17. The Last Seven Squares

After sixteen easy, not-so-easy and less-than-easy puzzles, the seventeenth and last is almost impossible – almost, of course, but not quite. If you found all the others fairly simple, this one shouldn't pose much of a problem for you. But if the others you found difficult, take a deep breath before you start on this one. You will need all 28 dominoes and you must use them to form seven squares, with 4 dominoes making up each square. Every square should look like this:

You won't be able to make the number of pips on all 28 sides of the seven squares come to the same total, but what you must do is make sure that the number of pips on each side of any one square is exactly the same. The joins don't have to match, unless you want them to – and if you want them to then you really are a domino demon who is ready to try the impossible! Good luck.

Solutions

1. First Square

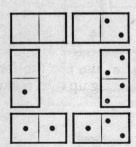

2. Second Square

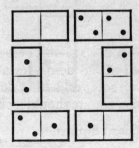

3. Triangular Trouble

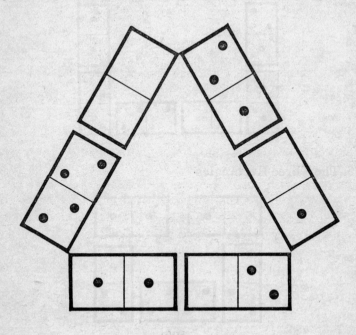

4. First Rectangle

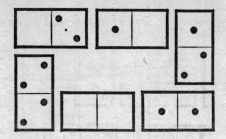

5. Giant Square

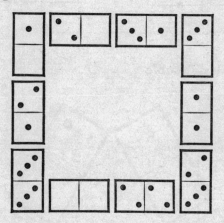

6. The Three Rectangles

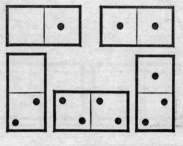

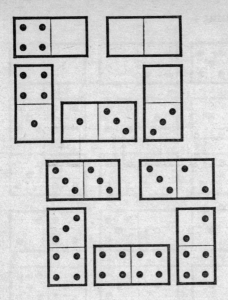

7. The Five Lines

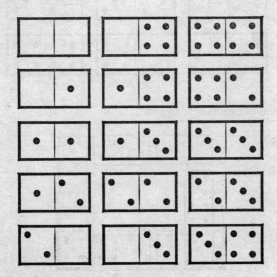

8. The Seven Lines

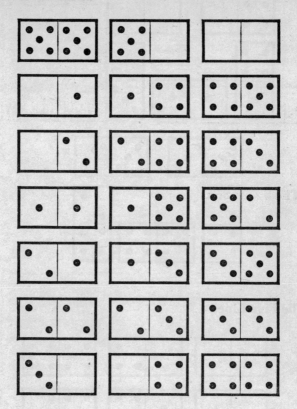

9. Three More Rectangles

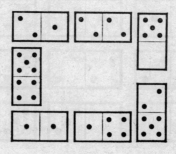

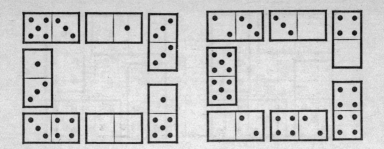

10. The Seven Squares

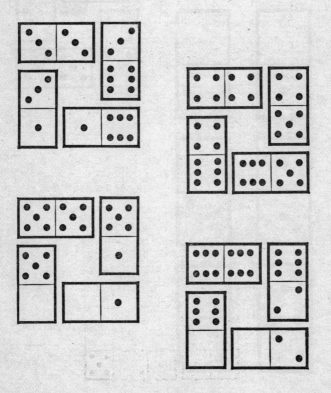

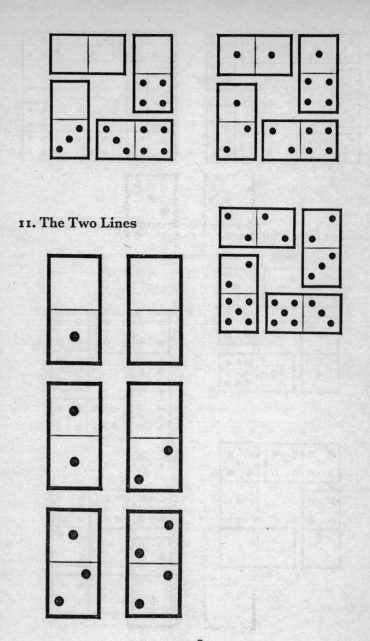

11. The Two Lines

12. The Two Columns

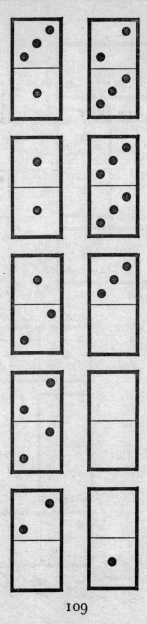

13. The Two Rectangles

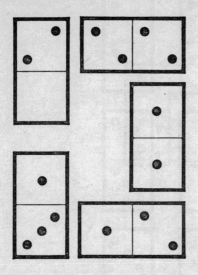

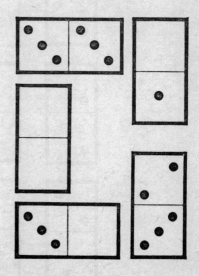

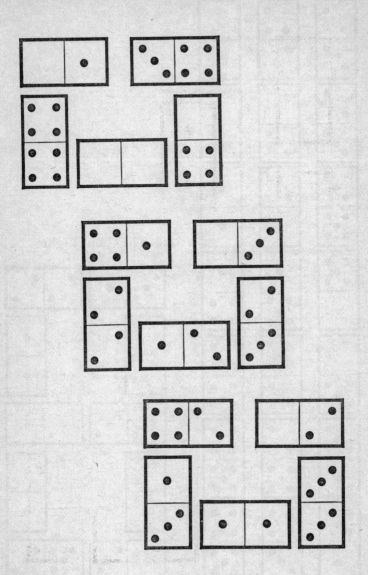

15. The Three Columns

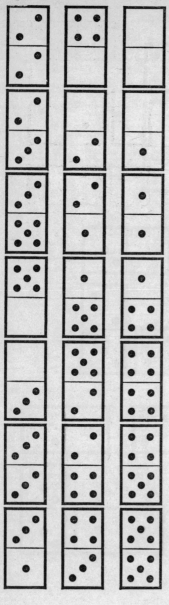

16. The Giant Eight

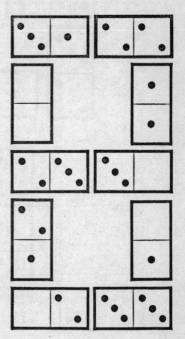

17. The Last Seven Squares

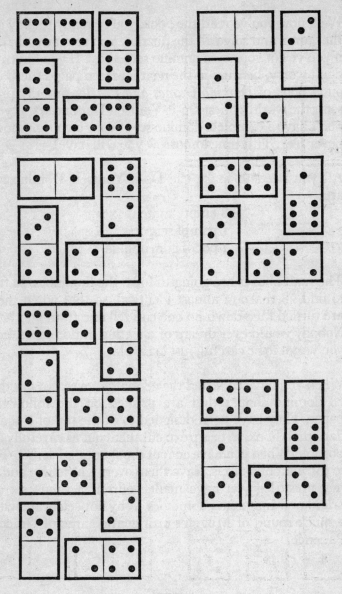

DO-IT-YOURSELF DOMINO SET

Well, now you've read the book, you're ready to play all the games and solve all the puzzles. You're ready, that is if you've got your own domino set handy. If you haven't, don't worry, because in the next fourteen pages the Carousel Book of *Domino Games and Puzzles* proudly presents the world's finest Do-it-Yourself Domino set. If you don't have a complete domino set of your own right now, never fear. This time tomorrow you will have!

All you need to make the Do-it-Yourself Domino set are:

> 28 empty matchboxes
> 1 pair of scissors
> 1 pot of gum or glue

The matchboxes are going to form the dominoes, so try to find 28 that are almost identical, so that when they are turned face-down no one can tell one from another. Nobody would ever dream of cheating at dominoes, but you've got to be careful, just in case!

When you have collected the 28 matchboxes, cut out the 28 domino shapes that are printed on the following pages. They have been designed to fit the top of a standard matchbox, so be sure to cut them out as carefully as possible. When you have cut out the shapes, stick them on to the matchbox tops, leave them overnight to dry and – hey presto! – you have made yourself a smart set of brand new matchbox dominoes. Why not celebrate with a quick round of Muggins or a gentle game of Grace's Patience?

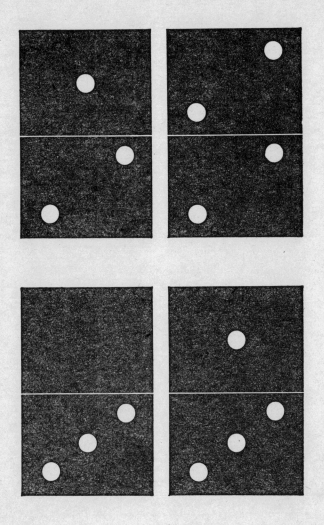

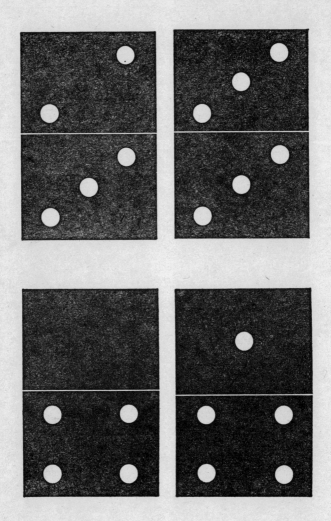

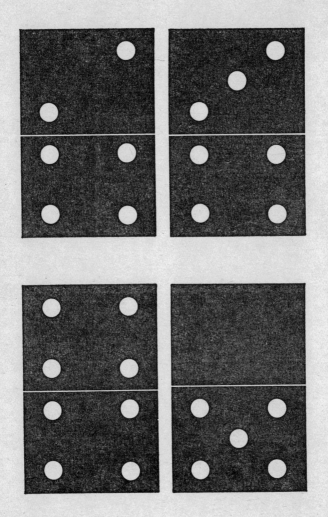

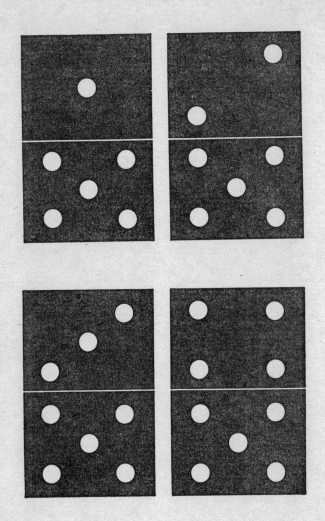

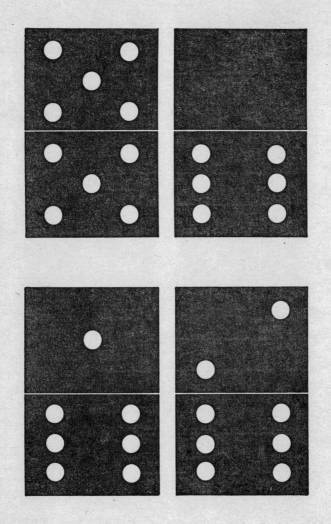

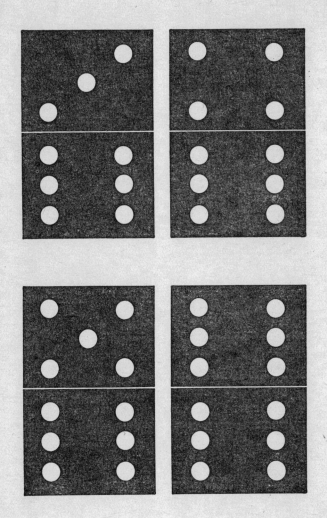

127